W9-AOD-147

HAVE YOU THANKED A KIDVENTOR TODAY?

BY
PATRICE
McLAURIN

Have You Thanked A KidVentor Today? by Patrice McLaurin

© 2019 by Patrice McLaurin. All rights reserved.
No part of this book may be reproduced in any written, electronic,
recording, or photocopying form without written permission of the author,
Patrice McLaurin, or the publisher, KhemRah Publishing, LLC.

Books may be purchased in quantity and/or special sales by contacting
the author at pmclaurin@patricemclaurin.com or the publisher at
sales@khemrahpublishing.com

Published by: KhemRah Publishing, LLC. Atlanta, GA.
Illustrated by: Dian Wang
Creative Director: Darren McLaurin

ISBN: 978-0-9973152-5-7
Library of Congress Control Number: 2019907296
MARC Org Code: GaBukP
1. Children's 2. Picture 3. History 4. Poetry 5. STEM
Second Edition

khemrahpublishing.com

Here's a fun fact about **_inventions_**:
Some of the world's coolest ideas have come from,
one of the most wondrous and inspiring places on earth,
a kid's imagination!

It's important to remember that children are **scholars**,

with beautiful minds, *eager* to learn new things.

If given the opportunity to share their *genius* with the world,

there's no limit to the joy kids can bring!

3

George Nissen is a perfect example.
He was an athlete and on the gymnastics team.
Which explains why during a fun day at the circus,
his eyes sparkled at the tumblers and their trapeze.
The **_trapeze artists_** would perform magical tricks in
the air then fall safely to their nets below.

George imagined it would be much more
exciting if they bounced up again and
continued with the show!

So with the help of his friends and a teacher,
he made the most brilliant thing!
By using iron scraps and tire tubing,
George invented the very first trampoline!

THANK YOU!

George Nissen

Then there's the story of Philo Farnsworth,
a farm boy who loved **_tinkering_** with things.
He'd take stuff apart just to see how it worked,
but his favorite interest was electricity.
One day, while working in the field he thought,
"I could use electrons to transmit images to a screen!"
This is really a fancy way of saying that little Philo
invented electronic TV!

Next we meet the incredible Robert Patch,
the youngest person to **_patent_** an invention!
He was 6 years old when he designed a toy that
has probably been played with by millions!

This curious and creative kindergartner
invented a very special toy truck.
It could change from a dump truck to a flatbed truck,
and back then, that was cool stuff!

That means he created two trucks in one!

He **_doubled_** his playtime and doubled his fun!

Not to mention, his invention has brought laughter,

joy and amusement to almost everyone!

THANK YOU!

Robert Patch

Of course we can't forget about Frank Epperson,
who made his invention by mistake.
His creation wasn't **_intentional_**,
yet he discovered something that was great!

Young Frank invented the Popsicle
when he was only 11 years old;
after preparing for himself a syrupy drink
that he left outside in the cold.

He arose the next morning,

after stretching and yawning,

from a long and peaceful night's sleep;

to a beautiful suprise, for before his eyes,

was a frozen treat that was easy to eat!

THANK YOU!
Frank Epperson

Now, some inventions make life a little easier.

The best inventions make life more fun.

There are also inventions that help to solve problems

when one needs to get something done.

So goes the tale of Chester Greenwood,
who as a kid, loved ice skating with friends.
But the ear flaps he wore
made his ears red and sore,
often bringing his fun to a quick end.

Chester realized his awful **_dilemma_**;

he enjoyed ice skating and didn't want to give it up.

So with the help of his grandma's sewing skills,

he invented modern day earmuffs!

THANK YOU!
Chester Greenwood

But what if the problem is that an inventor is too poor to buy the things that they need?

Well, that's when they tap into their brainpower to figure out a way to succeed.

Clever inventors don't always have money, but they have huge imaginations.

They're able to think of wonderful ideas to help improve their situation.

Take, for instance, William Kamkwamba.

His home had no electricity.

However, his village had plenty of wind that could produce ***clean energy***!

One day William discovered in a library book
awesome ways to make use of the wind.
He found that by building a **_windmill_**,
he could bring some of his energy problems to an end!

So he built his very first windmill; which powered light bulbs and charged cell phones.

In fact, it was William's inventiveness that provided electricity and water for his home!

THANK YOU!

William Kamkwamba

Then there is little Kelvin Doe.
Kelvin was only 11 years old,
when he started his own radio station to
help his community in Sierra Leone.
Kelvin was an *innovative* fellow
who used creativity to complete his task.
He even found the supplies that he needed
by bravely searching for them in the trash!

He made a **_generator_** for his radio station
and created batteries to power his home.
He produced enough batteries to share with
his neighbors, helping his community to develop and grow!
Kelvin had little money, but he was rich in intelligence.
He helped the people of his village with his
brain power and **_resourcefulness_**!

So the lesson to be learned from these stories is
that you are never too young,
to tap into the power and the ability
of your brilliant imagination!
If you can think it, you can invent it. All it takes is
determination, add in hard work, toss in **_initiative_**,
sprinkle on talent and top with **_inspiration_**!

And the fact of the matter is that it doesn't
matter if you are rich or if you are poor.
When that amazing idea pops into your head,
don't shiver with fear, instead explore it!
Put that big and beautiful brain to work,
you'll end up with something cool!
Who knows, maybe the next kidventor,
will be none other than you!

33

GLOSSARY

Clean Energy	— Energy that doesn't pollute (make dirty and unusable) the air or water
Dilemma	— A difficult situation where you must choose between two or more things
Double	— To cause something to become two times as great or as many
Eager	— Very excited and interested
Generator	— A machine that produces electricity
Genius	— A very smart or talented person
Initiative	— Deciding to do something on your own without being told to do so by someone else
Innovative	— Having new ideas about how something can be done
Inspiration	— Something or someone that makes some one want to do something or that gives an idea about what to do or create
Intentional	— Done in a way that is planned
Invention	— A useful new device or process

Patent	— A document that gives a person or company the right to be the only one that makes or sells a product
Resourceful	— Able to find solutions to problems
Scholar	— A very smart person or a student
Tinkering	— To try to repair or improve something
Trapeze artist	— A circus performer who performs tricks on a bar that is hung high above the ground by two ropes
Windmill	— A structure with blades that are moved by the wind and are used to produce electricity, pump water, etc.

Inflate
A BALLOON USING FIZZ!

Items Needed

- One (1) 16 oz empty plastic water bottle
- 1/2 cup of vinegar
- Baking soda
- Small balloon
- Piece of paper
- Tape

What to do

1. Take the piece of paper, roll it into the shape of a funnel then secure it with tape.
2. Slowly pour the vinegar into the bottle.
3. Stretch the balloon a few times to loosen it up. Then using the funnel you created, fill the balloon a little more than half way with baking soda.
4. Carefully place the neck of the balloon entirely over the neck of the bottle **without** letting any of the baking soda fall into the bottle.
5. Now, lift the balloon up so that the baking soda falls from the balloon into the bottle.
6. Watch as the baking soda mixes with the vinegar, creating the fizz that inflates the balloon!

Why This Works

The baking soda and the vinegar create an ACID-BASE reaction.
When these two chemicals mix together they create a gas called carbon dioxide.
Gasses need a lot of room to expand which is why after the carbon dioxide fills
the bottle it then moves into the balloon and inflates it!

I SHOULD ASK FOR HELP BEFORE DOING THESE
AWESOME EXPERIMENTS.

BUILD YOUR OWN ELECTROMAGNET

Items Needed

- A large iron nail (about 3 inches)
- About 3 feet of UNCOATED or THINLY COATED copper wire
- A fresh battery (any size will do)
- Some paper clips or other small magnetic objects
- An Adult (DO NOT ATTEMPT WITHOUT ADULT SUPERVISION)

What to do

1. Leaving about 5 inches of wire loose at one end, wrap the entire nail (as closely as possible) with wire, leaving about 5 inches of wire loose at the other end of the nail as well. Try not to overlap the wires.
2. If using coated wire, remove about an inch of the plastic coating from both ends of the wire (an adult is definitely needed for this step), if not, proceed to Step 3
3. Attach one of the loose wires to one end of a battery and the other loose wire to the other end of the battery. (It is best to tape the wires to the battery)
   CAUTION: There is a possibility that the wire could get very hot!
4. You now have an Electromagnet! Put the point of the nail near your paper clips or other small magnetic items and watch your new magnet pick them up!

DON'T FORGET TO DISCONNECT THE WIRES WHEN YOU ARE DONE WITH YOUR FUN!
AND NEVER PLACE THE WIRES NEAR A HOUSEHOLD OUTLET!

Why This Works

Most magnets are permanent magnets. A permanent magnet is a magnet that can't be turned off, similar to the ones that you may see on your grandmother's refrigerator. The magnet that you just made can be turned on and off, and is called an Electromagnet. Electromagnets run on electricity and are only magnetic when electricity is flowing. The electricity from the battery flows through the wire connected to the nail and rearranges the molecules in the nail so that they are attracted to certain metals. This is why your magnet can pick up small magnetic objects!

MAKE DELICIOUS ICE CREAM IN FIVE MINUTES

Items Needed

- 1 tablespoon sugar
- ½ cup milk
- ¼ teaspoon vanilla extract
- 6 tablespoons salt (Rock Salt or Kosher Salt is best but Table Salt will work)
- Ice (Enough to fill the gallon-sized bag halfway)
- 1 gallon-sized Ziploc bag
- 1 pint-sized Ziploc bag
- 1 Bowl

What to do

1. Fill the large (gallon sized) bag halfway with ice. Add the salt.
2. Mix the salt around in the ice and set aside.
3. Pour the milk, sugar and vanilla extract into the bowl and mix.
4. Pour the mixture into the small (pint sized) bag.
5. Close the bag with the mixture and make sure that it is completely sealed (You don't want to make a mess).
6. Bury the pint bag deep into the ice inside of the gallon bag.
7. Close the gallon bag and make sure that it is completely sealed (Again, you don't want to make a mess! This time you'd lose the entire treat if you did.).
8. Shake the bag as hard as you can for five minutes. If the bag is too cold and/or slippery, use a towel to hold the bag.

   After shaking, open the gallon sized bag, remove the pint sized bag and voila! You have your very own tasty frozen treat!

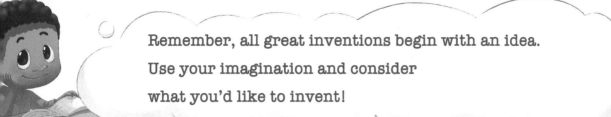

Remember, all great inventions begin with an idea.
Use your imagination and consider
what you'd like to invent!

WHAT WOULD YOU LIKE TO INVENT?

DIRECTIONS: Using your imagination, brainstorm and think of an invention that you would like to invent. Your invention should make life easier, safer or more fun! Answer the questions below to help you with your brainstorming:

1. What is the name of your invention?_____

2. What does your invention do?_____

_____

_____

3. How will your invention make life easier, safer or more fun? _____

_____

_____

4. What inspired you to create this invention? _____

_____

_____

About the Author

Patrice McLaurin is an award winning author, youth motivational speaker and character education consultant. She enjoys a good game of Scrabble and loves to read an exciting thriller! Her first children's book, "Have You Thanked an Inventor Today?" was acclaimed by Microsoft as a book that inspires STEM. It also received the 5 Star Rating Award from Reader's Favorite.

Her latest book, "Have You Thanked a KidVentor Today?" is another engaging STEM read that highlights some of the wonderful contributions of child inventors. The goal of the book is to encourage children to recognize and tap into their own ingenious inclinations.

Patrice McLaurin is a native of Bessemer, AL and a proud graduate of Alabama A&M University. She currently resides in Lawrenceville, GA with her husband and two children.

patricemclaurin.com
facebook.com/thankaninventor
instagram.com/patricemclaurin
twitter.com/mclaurinwrites
pmclaurin@patricemclaurin.com

Sources

Doe Kelvin

Sengeh, David. "DIY Africa: Empowering a New Sierra Leone." CNN. November 14, 2012. Accessed January 12, 2018. https://cnn.it/2HIJ6Ds.

"Kelvin Doe, Self-Taught Engineering Whiz from Sierra Leone, Wows MIT Experts." Huffington Post. November 30, 2012. Accessed January 12, 2018. https://bit.ly/2umKOTm.

Grant, Valerie. "Persistent Experimentation - Kelvin Doe." TEDxTeen. December 30, 2016. Accessed January 13, 2018. https://bit.ly/2Fqx8wF

Chu, Jeff. "The Philanthropic Prodigy." Fast Company. May 13, 2013. Accessed January 12, 2018. https://bit.ly/2JvceAO

McFadden, Christopher. "Whatever Happened to Child Prodigy Kelvin Doe." Interesting Engineering. October 18, 2016. Accessed January 14, 2018. https://bit.ly/2TqlndA.

Epperson, Frank

Pope, S. "How an 11 Year Old Boy Invented the Popsicle". NPR. July 22, 2015. Accessed January 12, 2018. https://n.pr/2ESJmwm.

Fiegel, A. "A Brief History of Popsicles." Smithsonian Magazine. July 7, 2010. Accessed January 12, 2018. https://bit.ly/2Fr6EvO.

Moak, Jefferson. "The Frozen Sucker War: Good Humor v. Popsicle."Prologue Magazine. Spring 2005. Volume 37. No. 1. Accessed January 12, 2018. https://bit.ly/2TqbYTa.

"Popsicle." How Products Are Made. Encyclopedia.com. Accessed January 13, 2018. https://bit.ly/2UJR1nP.

Epperson, F. W. (1924). United States Patent. US001505592. Retrieved from https://bit.ly/2JxtsgT.

Farnsworth, Philo

Sampaolo, M. "Philo Farnsworth." Lemelson – MIT. Accessed January 12, 2018. https://bit.ly/2TON7xG.

"Philo T. Farnsworth." Encyclopedia of World Biography. . Accessed January 12, 2018. https://bit.ly/2Fi18JV.

"The TV Guy."Utah Division of State History. Accessed January 12, 2018. https://bit.ly/2WftvQ4.

Gregerson, E."Philo Farnsworth, American Inventor."Britannica.com. Accessed January 12, 2018. https://bit.ly/2dceRUl.

Farnsworth, P.T. (1936). United States Patent. US002037711. Retrieved from https://bit.ly/2Tsx2bI.

Greenwood, Chester

McCarthy, M.   Earmuffs for Everyone! How Chester Greenwood Became Known as the Inventor of Earmuffs. (New York, NY: Simon and Schuster, 2015)

Esher, Kat. "The Teenager Who Patented Earmuffs Kept His Town Employed for 60 Years.". Smithsonian Magazine. March 13, 2017. Accessed January 12, 2018. https://bit.ly/2HwUyPt.

Porter, Nancy. "Chester Greenwood."Accessed January 12, 2018. https://bit.ly/2YdwiLd, https://bit.ly/2TZbnfL.

Lipman, Don. "The Story of the Modern-Day Earmuff and Its Inventor, Chester Greenwood. Washington Post. March 2, 2016. Accessed January 12, 2018. https://wapo.st/2TmBFE7.

Greenwood, C. (1877). United States Patent. US000188292. Retrieved from https://bit.ly/2Tr7DiP.

Sources

Kamkwamba, William

Kamwamba, W. "About William." Accessed January 12, 2018. https://bit.ly/2IVqVrW.

Sheerin, J."Malawi Windmill Boy With Big Fans." BBC News. October 1, 2009. Accessed January 14, 2018. https://bbc.in/1wYJFj9.

Kamwamba, W. "How I Built a Windmill, " filmed 2007. TED Talk video. Accessed January 14, 2018. from https://bit.ly/1H2lTB6.

Kamkwamba, W., Mealer, B. The Boy Who Harnessed the Wind: Creating Currents of Electricity and Hope.
(New York, NY: William Morrow, 2009)

Nissen, George

Kennedy, P. "Who Made That Trampoline?". New York Times. September 28, 2012. Accessed January 12, 2018. https://nyti.ms/2WcuH6x.

Bertz, J. "Excerpts From a 2006 Interview With George Nissen" USA Gym. January 2006.Accessed January 13, 2018. https://bit.ly/2FrGPep.

Dagmur, M. "My Father's Dream of an Olympic Trampoline: Life Story of George Nissen, Inventor of the Trampoline." (Tuscan, AZ: Wheatmark, 2012).

"Trampoline." How Products Are Made. Encyclopedia.com.Accessed January 13, 2018. https://bit.ly/2JvOEUA.

Nissen, G.P. (1966). United States Patent. US003256021. Retrieved from https://bit.ly/2U2Jx2a.

Patch, Robert

Proffitt, S. (2013 June 4). "50 Years Later, Robert Patch Remembers Being Youngest Person With a US Patent." Southern California Public Radio. Juner 4, 2013.Accessed January 13, 2018. https://bit.ly/2HMumU4.

Sprung, S."10 Incredible Things Invented By Kids." Business Insider. June 15, 2012.Accessed January 12, 2018. https://bit.ly/2HMxLCl.

Putnal, O. "7 Things You Didn't Know Were Invented By Kids". Woman's Day Magazine Online. May 18, 2010.Accessed January 12, 2018. https://bit.ly/2lpunjg.

Whitman, A. Ideas, Boys Life, Volume 58. (1968), pp. 15.

Patch, R.W. (1963). United States Patent. US003091888. Retrieved from https://bit.ly/2OnEhAP.

CPSIA information can be obtained
at www.ICGtesting.com
Printed in the USA
LVHW071731120822
725820LV00002B/42

9 780997 315257